# BOOK ANALYSIS

By Maria Aalto

# The Ministry of Utmost Happiness

BY ARUNDHATI ROY

Bright
≡Summaries.com

# ARUNDHATI ROY

## INDIAN WRITER

- **Born in Shillong, Meghalaya, India in 1961.**
- **Notable works:**
  - *The God of Small Things* (1997), novel
  - *The Algebra of Infinite Justice* (2001), an essay collection
  - *Listening to Grasshoppers: Field Notes on Democracy* (2009), an essay collection

Arundhati Roy is an Indian writer of fiction and non-fiction. She is best known for her novel *The God of Small Things*, for which she won the Man Booker Prize in 1997.

Roy is a writer and an activist. After her first novel, *The God of Small Things,* she concentrated on writing non-fiction and produced several volumes of essays which explore social problems in India and around the world. She speaks out on issues related to topics such as race, class, the caste system in India, gender, political power and environmental problems. Like her essays and her first novel, her highly anticipated second novel, *The Ministry of Utmost Happiness*, published 20 years after *The God of Small Things*, also explores social problems without being afraid to discuss sensitive issues such as the conflicts between separatist Muslims in Kashmir and the Indian government. Roy is outspoken and her writing style is intelligent and direct. Her fiction is written in a lyrical style and she uses fragmented, non-linear narratives to patch together complex stories.

# THE MINISTRY OF UTMOST HAPPINESS

## AN EXPLORATION OF CONTEMPORARY INDIA

- **Genre:** novel
- **Reference edition:** Roy, A. (2018) *The Ministry of Utmost Happiness*. London: Penguin Books.
- **1ˢᵗ edition:** 2017
- **Themes:** love, motherhood, gender, identity, Indian society, caste system, conflict in Kashmir

*The Ministry of Utmost Happiness* is set in contemporary India. It patches together various narratives, most importantly those of Tilo and Anjum. Anjum is an intersex person looking for her place in the world. Although, physically, her male characteristics are dominant and her parents raise her as a boy, Anjum identifies as a woman. She joins a community of hijras, transgender women. Later she starts to live in the graveyard, where she runs a guesthouse and organises funeral services for other people who do not fit into society. Anjum dreams of motherhood and her story becomes entangled with that of Tilo, a restless, independent woman who is loved by three men, when Tilo claims an abandoned baby as her own.

The novel examines contemporary India, investigating its different classes, castes, religions, conflicts and historical events. Anjum and Tilo's stories give life to different aspects of Indian society.

# SUMMARY

## ANJUM

The novel, which is mainly set in Delhi, is made up of the interconnected stories of different characters. The first sections of the book focus on Anjum, a transgender/intersex individual who lives in a graveyard. She lives isolated from her society.

When Anjum was born, she was thought to be a boy and was named Aftab. When her mother discovers that Aftab also has a kind of vagina (although physically her male characteristics are dominant), she is shocked, but tells no-one. When years later her father finds out, they try to seek medical help for the 'problem'. Aftab is raised as a boy, but when she sees a hijra, a transgender woman, she wants to be like her. She starts to spend time at the 'Khwabgah', a home to the local community of hijras, and when she is old enough, she runs away from home and joins the community.

After years spent at the Khwabgah, one day Anjum finds an abandoned little girl and brings her home with her. Anjum becomes very attached to the girl, called Zainab, who starts to call her mummy. The other members of the community also help look after her. Zainab is often sick and Anjum is very worried. She even suspects that Saeeda, a younger member of the community (who calls herself a transperson, rather than using the traditional term hijra) is causing the illnesses. Saeeda is unaware of these suspicions, and likes both Anjum and Zainab. When seeking spiritual guidance for the problem, Anjum is advised to visit the dargah (shrine) of Hazrat Gharib Nawaz. She makes the journey to Ahmedabad with Zakir Mian, a friend of her father. They are caught up in the violence that starts with the killings of Hindu pilgrims and results in violence against Muslims as a 'reaction' (Anjum is a Muslim). Anjum is brought back home, but Zakir Mian is not found. Anjum does not speak of her experiences, but she is changed. She finally leaves the Khwabgah and begins her lonely existence at the graveyard. Zainab stays at the Khwabgah with Saeeda.

## ANJUM'S GUESTHOUSE

Although Anjum lives alone now, those close to her visit her at the graveyard, and she makes friends with Ziauddin, an old imam. Her lonely, simple existence is slowly transformed, as she makes the graveyard her home and begins constructing accommodation there. She finally runs a guest house, where she welcomes other people who are rejected by their society. She accommodates Saddam Hussain, originally called Dayachanda, a young man of Hindu origin whose family belongs to the lowest caste. He was deeply affected by his father being killed by a mob when he was falsely accused of killing a cow. Motivated by (the real) Saddam Hussain's calm when facing death, he decides to become a Muslim and take his name. He plans to avenge his father's death, and wants to face the consequences with the same courage. Anjum tells him that Saddam Hussain killed many people, but he still admires the original Saddam Hussain's courage.

One day Saddam, Anjum and some of their friends are out in Delhi observing different kinds of activists protesting. A baby is found on the pavement. Anjum, who badly wants a child, wants to take the baby, but people disagree on what to do with it. In the meanwhile, an unknown woman leaves with the baby. They manage to find the woman and the baby later.

## GARSON HOBART

The next, larger section of the novel is written from the perspective of Biplab Dasgupta, the landlord and a friend of Tilo, the woman who took the baby. He has always loved Tilo, although they have never been a couple, and he is married and has two daughters. He has recently returned from Kabul, and finds out that Tilo has not been in her apartment for a while (she is at Anjum's guesthouse). He first met Tilo in 1984, when they were students and were rehearsing a play called 'Norman, Is That You?' together with their friends Naga and Musa. Tilo always calls Biplab Garson Hobart, which is his character in the play. Naga and Biplab are both from privileged Hindu families, while Musa is a Muslim from Kashmir. Tilo's mother was a Christian from a respectable family, but was shunned by her family because she had Tilo out of wedlock and in secret from her society, left her to an orphanage and returned to adopt her, but never admitted that she was her biological child. This makes Tilo's family background complicated, and as a result she is an unusually independent young woman. Tilo and Musa were previously in a relationship. Biplab has very little contact with the two of them for many years, until Tilo needs his help.

Biplab works for the government, and is in Kashmir for his work during conflicts that result from the Kashmiri separatist movement. He receives a phone call from Major Amrik Singh, a violent, influential member of the army, telling him that a lady whom they captured with a militant has asked to give him the following message: G.A.R.S.O.N. H.O.B.A.R.T. He knows it is Tilo and sends Naga, who is working as journalist with connections to the government, to get her. They assume that the militant, whom she was with and who was killed by the soldiers, to have been Musa. Tilo and Naga go back to Delhi, where they are later married. They stay together for 14 years until Tilo leaves Naga. She then rents the apartment from Biplab.

## TILO

The next section focuses on Tilo's experiences. The events told from Biplab's perspective are told as Tilo lived them. She had been together with Musa, but they have now gone their separate ways. She has been living alone for years when she hears of Musa and goes to meet him in the conflict-ridden Kashmir. She stays on a house boat with Gulrez, Musa's friend. Musa tells Tilo about his life and sends her exploring Kashmir with his friends as guides, so that she understands what motivates him and others like him who are involved with the separatist movement. Tilo learns that Musa had been married and had had a daughter, but both his wife and his daughter had been killed amidst the violence during one of the many conflicts in the area. After losing his family Musa has become more involved with the movement. Tilo and Musa still have feelings towards each other, and they understand each other at a profound level.

Soon after Musa has said his goodbyes and left Tilo on the house boat, before she returns to Delhi the government soldiers come, take Tilo and Gulrez into custody and try to find Musa. The soldiers kill Gulrez, claiming to have killed Musa. Tilo gets help from Biplab and Naga. She later sees Musa again before going back to Delhi, and he advises her not to be alone, for protection, and maybe to marry someone, which is what she does. In Delhi she discovers she is pregnant with Musa's baby, but opts for abortion because she does not want the child to suffer in the difficult circumstances. Years later, however, she takes the abandoned baby, and names her Miss Jebeen to honour the memory of Musa's daughter.

## THE MINISTRY OF UTMOST HAPPINESS

Tilo has taken Anjum's offer and now lives with Anjum and Miss Jebeen the Second at the graveyard. Everyone is happy with the arrangement. Saddam Hussain and Zainab, now a grown-up, get married. Musa, who has kept in contact with Tilo, even if irregularly, over the years, visits her one last time, before she hears he has died in the conflict. Tilo feels at home in Anjum's graveyard guesthouse even after Musa's death because she feels a spiritual connection there, and Anjum feels happy with her child and other people around her.

# CHARACTER STUDY

## ANJUM

Anjum is an intersex individual who was raised as a boy, but who identifies as female. When she sees a transgender woman at the market place, she "want[s] to be her" (p. 18). She joins a community of hijras, or transgender women. While she finds some happiness in expressing her femininity, it is not enough to give her fulfilment. She finds this in motherhood and helping other people who are struggling. Anjum mothers Zainab, and abandoned little girl she found on the street, until she is changed by her experience of being caught in the middle of a massacre that her travel companion did not survive, and she feels the need to leave her community. Zainab stays in the care of Saeeda, another woman in the community, which is heartbreaking for Anjum. She now lives in the graveyard, initially unkept and alone, but finally connects with other people who need help and with her friends. She runs a guesthouse and arranges funeral services from the graveyard, providing services to those who have been rejected from other places. When Tilo claims the abandoned baby as her own, Anjum reaches out to her, and is given a second opportunity to be a mother. Nothing is as important to Anjum as becoming a mother. She is goodhearted, but also impulsive and a little quick-tempered. She is also strongminded and knows what she wants. She belongs to an older generation of transgender women, and prefers the traditional Indian term hijra.

## TILO

Tilo is an intelligent and independent woman with a unique background. Her biological mother adopted her and raised her as her adoptive daughter because she was born out of wedlock. She does not have much contact with her mother until she is dying and she goes to look after her. As she has no family to help her, she has become used to taking care of herself. She lives her life as she pleases and does not attempt to please anyone with the choices she makes or with her appearance. Nevertheless, three men love her: Musa, Biplab and Naga. Musa is the love of her life, but she had broken off their relationship in the past because of her need for freedom and because of her restlessness. When she goes to meet Musa later, they continue the relationship, but the difficulties caused by the conflicts in Kashmir keep them apart. Tilo marries Naga, not out of love (although she feels some affection for him), but for protection. Her restlessness causes her to leave Naga too. She only finds peace after she has taken (kidnapped) the abandoned child on the street and moved with the child to live at Anjum's guesthouse. Here, surrounded by other social outcasts, and feeling a spiritual connection with the otherworld, she feels at home. Here she is not undone even by the grief of Musa's death because she is able to communicate with him through "the crack in the door that the battered angels in the graveyard held open (illegally) for her" (p. 437).

## BIPLAB DASGUPTA

Biplab Dasgupta is Tilo's landlord who has loved her since they were young. He says that he had no hope with Tilo, not only because she did not love him, but also because his parents would not have accepted her, "the girl without a past, without a caste" (p. 161). He is an upper caste Hindu (Brahmin). He has lived a privileged life and has done what has been expected of him: he has married a woman who belongs to his caste and works for the government. He does not blindly believe in the government's cause in Kashmir, and recognises that horrible acts of violence are committed on both sides. Nevertheless, he says that "If one *has* to choose, then give me a Hindu fundamentalist any day over a Muslim one" (p. 194). However, after spending time going through Tilo's papers in her apartment and after losing his job and his family because of his drinking, he has had time to think things over, and he comes to the conclusion that the Kashmiris are right.

## NAGA

Naga is an upper caste Hindu man. He and Biplab are friends and rivals. He changes his looks and personalities many times to suit his opinions and circumstances. He is a charismatic man and many women find him attractive. He works as a journalist. He is intelligent and can argue well for his opinions, but does not commit to anything or anyone, except when he marries Tilo. She, in turn, cannot commit to him, as she is restless by nature and loves Musa. Naga is heartbroken when Tilo leaves him, but tries to continue his life.

## MUSA

Musa is the love of Tilo's life, but they have spent most of their lives apart, first because of Tilo's unwillingness to commit and then because of the difficult circumstances caused by the conflict in Kashmir. He is a Kashmiri Muslim and is involved with the separatist movement. Musa is a quiet, at times serious man, who cares deeply for his people. He loved his wife and daughter dearly, and is deeply affected by their deaths. He and Tilo share a special bond; they love, respect and understand each other in way no-one else can. He understands Tilo's need for independence and respects her need to be in control of her life. He tells her: "We'll win this war, and then we'll be together, you and I. I'll wear a hijab [...] and you can take up arms" (p. 389).

## SADDAM HUSSAIN

Saddam Hussain is originally a Hindu from the lowest social class possible; he is one of those formally known as 'untouchables'. His father is killed by a mob after they are arrested, wrongly accused of killing a cow. In reality, their work was to dispose of cow carcasses for the upper caste Hindus. Deeply traumatised by this event, Saddam, who was originally called Dayachanda, takes up his unusual name and becomes a Muslim. He wants to avenge his father and admires the original Saddam Hussain's courage in the face of death. He says: "I want to be this kind of a bastard, [...] I want to do what I have to do and then, if I have to pay a price, I want to pay it like that" (p. 91). However, finally, Saddam does not commit any violence to avenge his father because he is satisfied with his social class rising against their oppressors. He marries Zainab, the first abandoned child Anjum took under her wing. He and Zainab share a love for animals.

## ZAINAB

Anjum finds the lost or abandoned Zainab and takes her home with her. Zainab initially calls

Anjum 'mummy', but finally stays under Saeeda's care at the Khwabgah when Anjum leaves it and moves to the graveyard. She does not, however, disappear from Anjum's life. She visits her at the graveyard (although there is long period of time when it is too difficult for her and Anjum), and finally marries Anjum's friend, Saddam Hussain. She is a strong-willed young woman who loves fashion and animals.

## MAJOR AMRIK SINGH

Major Amrik Singh is a cruel member of the government forces. He tortures and kills without remorse. He intimidates Musa's family and is behind Tilo's arrest and Gulrez's death. The government cannot control him, and after he is involved with the killing of human rights activist, he kills everyone who wanted to testify against him. He cannot continue in the army after this, but he cannot be brought to justice either, because he knows too much. It is decided that he must apply for asylum in the U.S. under false claims of persecution in his country, which he does, only to finally kill himself and his family in the U.S., because the Kashmiris make it known that they know where he is and have not for-gotten what he has done.

## MISS JEBEEN THE SECOND

Miss Jebeen the Second, the baby whom Tilo finds, is named after Musa's dead daughter. She makes Tilo and Anjum happy. Her new mothers receive a letter from the biological mother, who is now dead, explaining her difficult life as a social outcast and a communist and how her child was conceived as a result of a gang rape. She could not and did not want to care for the child, but hopes that someone else will provide the child with the nurturing she could not. Caring for her fulfils Anjum's dreams of motherhood.

# ANALYSIS

## A POSTCOLONIAL NOVEL

*The Ministry of Utmost Happiness* can be described as a postcolonial novel. Postcolonialism is a complex term with many possible definitions, but it can be broadly described by saying that it "deals with the effects of colonization on cultures and societies" (Ashcroft et al., 2013: 190). The novel is set in postcolonial India and deals with the social problems in this setting. Many layers of modern postcolonial India are mentioned and explored in the book: the formal colonial power and modern Western tourists are described and compared to Indian people and customs, and contemporary India is explored in all its complexity. The difficulty of building a nation made up of many different ethnic, social and religious groups is at the centre of the novel.

## CONTEMPORARY INDIAN SOCIETY

*The Ministry of Utmost Happiness* explores many social problems in contemporary India. The problems investigated and exposed are not limited to those caused by colonialism (which by no means should be taken as a sign of downplaying the seriousness of the impact of colonialism), but also include other social problems such as poverty and the injustice of the Hindu caste system. Baul and Sanasam discuss the social activism in Roy's work (prior to *The Ministry of Utmost Happiness*) and remark that "Roy always has a cry for the poor, the 'Dalit', Women and the discriminated one within the society" (Baul and Sanasam, 2014: 35). Their observation is true for this novel too. Characters such as Saddam Hussain, who is at the bottom of the social hierarchy, exemplify the hardships people of his social status suffer. As a political activist, Roy not only exposes the suffering of her lower caste characters; she also shows their defiance and their struggle for social justice. Saddam refuses to live as a victim. He takes his destiny into his own hands, and is happy when he sees other people of his social class rising against their oppressors. Other problems in Indian society include conflicts between followers of different religions, particularly Hindus and Muslims. These tensions are heightened in the post-9/11 world. The characters watch the terrorist attack on TV and try to make sense of it (pp. 40-41). These events complicate the lives of the Muslim characters in an already divided India.

## KASHMIR

The most poignant example of conflict between different groups in India is Kashmir's militant struggle for independence. Kashmir is mainly inhabited by Muslims, and they want independence from the Hindu-ruled India. The struggle is violent and complicated. Clark observes that "as a campaigner for Kashmiri independence, Roy is more than alive to its complexities" (Clark, 2017). She describes the situation with sympathy for the Kashmiri cause, but without painting Indians as the enemy, and without forgetting that Kashmiri society too is divided, that there are different schools of thought among Muslims, and that the freedom Kashmiri militants fight for can mean very different things to them. While there are very negative characters on the side of the Indian government, such as Major Amrik Singh, who is violent and ruthless, there are also characters such Biplab, who is merely doing his job working for the government, and whose patriotic feelings regarding the issue seem lukewarm at most. In fact, although he first criticises violence on both sides but states that he prefers Hindu fundamentalists to Muslim fundamentalists (p. 194), he finally starts to sympathise with the Kashmiri cause. During his last meeting with Musa he says that "You may be right after all" (p. 431). Roy's commitment to the Kashmiri cause is best seen through Musa, who is described in a very positive light. Musa is intelligent, caring, respectful and courageous. He dies for his cause and for his community. Moreover, the deaths of his wife and his little girl call for empathy from the reader. The Kashmiri continue their struggle and Roy shows her support for it in this novel.

## POVERTY

Poverty is frequently mentioned in *The Ministry of Utmost Happiness*. This is exemplified through the experiences of the Dalits (formally known as untouchables) as discussed earlier, but also through the experiences of poor Muslims, Christians and everyone else who is not part of the social elite. Hunger, lack of shelter, clean water and other basic needs are among the problems faced by so many people in India, as Roy demonstrates on several occasions in the novel. One example of the misery suffered by poor people is what Tilo hears on TV one night:

> "homeless people had taken to sleeping on the edges of roads with heavy traffic. They had discovered that diesel exhaust fumes from passing trucks and buses were an effective mosquito repellent and protected them from the outbreak of dengue fever that had killed several hundred people in the city already" (p. 256)

The sheer desperation of these people exposes the deprivation that India's most unprivileged people live in. This and many other examples like it constantly remind the reader of the fate of the people who have absolutely nothing.

## GENDER

Another social issue problematised in the novel is gender. The issues include gender inequality between men and women, as well as the social problems faced by transpeople or the hijra, the Indian third gender. Anjum and other hijras live in their own communities, at the margins of society. However, these characters are not described as sad victims, but as strongminded individuals, actively seeking empowerment. For example, when Anjum (or Aftab, as she was still called at the time) first observes another hijra, Bombay Silk, she is described as a beautiful, powerful person who can do what ordinary women cannot (pp. 18-19). This does not mean that Roy does not problematise their place at the margins of society, but that they can and should be empowered. The fact that Anjum, an older hijra, fulfils her dream of becoming a mother is a powerful message about what can be possible for someone like her.

Tilo represents another type of emancipation regarding gender inequality. Gender roles are still rather traditional in India and a character like her is a token of female empowerment. She is very intelligent and independent and shows what an Indian woman can achieve. The fact that she does not have a powerful family behind her is both a blessing and a curse. On the one hand, Tilo is very much alone in the world without help from the family, and on the other hand, she does not have a family telling her how to live her life, and she learns from her struggles. Tilo does not attempt to please anyone, and makes her own choices. Her freedom is important to her, and she does not want to give it up, even for the sake of the man she loves. It is significant that Musa understands and respects this, and tells her that when they are together, he will be the one who will "wear a hijab" (p. 389). While this is playful (and absolutely does not mean that Musa does not respect Muslim traditions), Roy shows with this not only the importance of female emancipation, but also men's role in changing attitudes for achieving greater equality.

## STYLE

The most important stylistic elements of *The Ministry of Utmost Happiness* are the use of different types of narrators, fragmented, non-linear narration and a poetic style.

Most of the novel is told by a third-person omniscient narrator, who can tell the reader how the numerous characters experience the events described. The narrator focuses on different characters in different passages. In addition to this, there are passages told from the point of view of Biplab Dasgupta, as a first-person narrative.

His narrative perspective differs remarkably from the third-person narrator, which shows the multitude of interpretations possible for the same events, as well as how the narrator's knowledge affects the narration. For example, as he assumes that Musa has died when Tilo is captured by the soldiers, his vision of the events that follow is very different from that of the third-person narrator who knows that Musa is still alive and in contact with Tilo. Using the two types of narrators in combination supports the complex, fragmented structure of the novel.

This fragmented structure is the novel's other striking stylistic feature. The novel is non-linear and made up of the stories of different characters. Roy weaves the stories together to form a complex whole that shows how seemingly separate stories can become connected. The most obvious example of this is how Tilo and Anjum's stories become connected when they want to claim the same abandoned child as theirs. Tilo and Anjum's experiences until that point are separate but become interconnected as life has prepared them both to be women who wish to take the abandoned baby under their wing.

The novel's fragmented style, its interconnected stories and social awareness are further supported by its poetic style. Roy uses poetic images and lines of poetry to intensify the novel's content. For example, Anjum is described as living "in the graveyard like a tree" (p. 3). This poetic image roots Anjum to her environment and gives her unorthodox existence dignity. Regarding the use of lines of poetry, Anjum's father, for example, likes to recite poetry. The following couplets by the Urdu poet Mir Taqi Mir are given in Urdu and in English in the novel:

> "Jis sar ko ghurur aaj hai yaan taj-vari ka
> Kal uss pe yahin shor hai phir nauhagari ka
> The head which today proudly flaunts a crown
> Will tomorrow, right here, in lamentation drown" (p. 15)

These lines both anchor the novel in Indian culture and support its social messages. There are many other quotations like this, which intensify the experience of reading the book.

# FURTHER REFLECTION

## SOME QUESTIONS TO THINK ABOUT...

- Discuss the social problems highlighted in the novel. How do the fictional elements support the exploration of the social problems in contemporary India?
- How are the different Indian religious groups represented in the novel?
- Discuss the transgender characters (or hijras) in the novel. What is their role in Indian society and how do the different generations of hijras differ from one another (compare, for example, Anjum and Saeeda)?
- In your opinion, why does Anjum leave the Khwabgah?
- Compare the three men in Tilo's life. What are their functions in the novel?
- In your opinion, why does Tilo take the baby?
- How would you interpret the novel's title?
- In your opinion, do the different fragments of the novel form a whole that works? Why (not)?
- Discuss the use of poetry in the novel. What is its impact?

*We want to hear from you!*
*Leave a comment on your online library*
*and share your favourite books on social media!*

# FURTHER READING

## REFERENCE EDITION

- Roy, A. (2018) *The Ministry of Utmost Happiness*. London: Penguin Books.

## REFERENCE STUDIES

- Ashcroft et al. (2013) *Post-Colonial Studies: The Key Concepts*. New York: Routledge.

- Baul, A. & Sansam, R. (2014). Study of Social Activism in Arundhati Roy's work. *Journal of Humanities and Social Science (IOSR-JHSS)*. 19 (1), pp. 35-38.

- Clark, A. (2017) The Ministry of Utmost Happiness by Arundhati Roy review – a patchwork of narratives. *The Guardian*. [Online]. [Accessed 24 January 2019]. Available from: <https://www.theguardian.com/books/2017/jun/11/ministry-utmost-happiness-arundhati-roy-review>

- Flynn et al. (2006). Arundhati Roy. *University of Minnesota*. [Online]. [Accessed 24 January 2019]. Available from: <https://conservancy.umn.edu/bitstream/handle/11299/166316/Roy,%20Arundhati.pdf;sequence=1>

## MORE FROM BRIGHTSUMMARIES.COM

- Reading guide – *The God of Small Things* by Arundhati Roy.

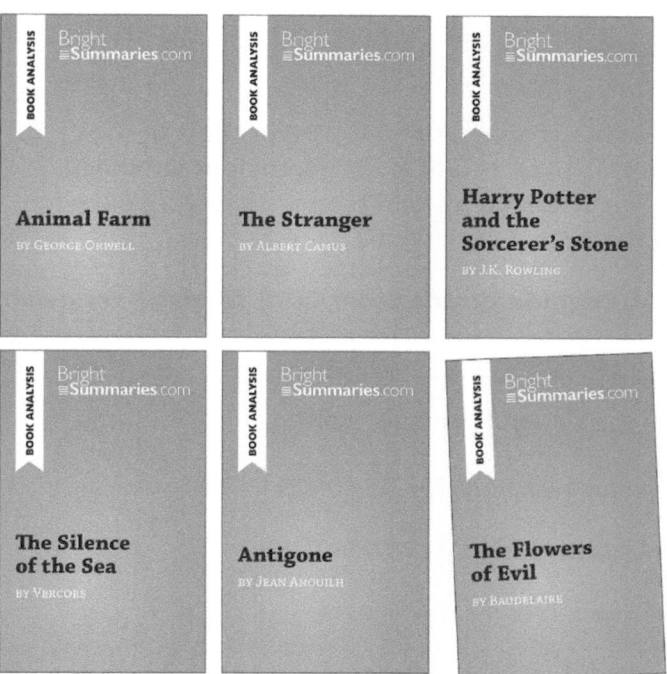

www.brightsummaries.com

Ebook EAN: 9782808017527

Paperback EAN: 9782808017534

Legal Deposit: D/2019/12603/43

Cover: © Primento

Digital conception by Primento, the digital partner of publishers.